MW01633488

Fitness for People with

Heart Problems

Fitness for People with

Heart Problems

Bryce Taylor

Fitzhenry & Whiteside

Editor: Frank English
Composition and Design: Jay Tee Graphics
Drawings: Jay Tee Graphics

Printed and bound in Canada

Canadian Cataloguing in Publication Data
Tayor, Bryce, 1933-
   Fitness for people with heart problems

Bibliography: p.
ISBN 0-88902-529-0
1. Cardiacs - Rehabilitation.   2. Exercise therapy.
I. Title.

RC684.E9T39 1986   616.1'2062   C86-099166-8

Acknowledgements

Special thanks are due to the people and institutions listed below, for their
considerable assistance in the preparation of this book:

The past and present doctors and staff of Toronto Western Hospital, especially
Dr. Baird, Dr. Beanland, Dr. Petkovich, and Dr. David. To Dr. Stecyk for his
continued support; Bernice Morrison and Kuli Miller, researchers. To Eric
Willis, Earle Berger, Russ Kisby, and Dr. Harold Minden for their helpful
comments. The Fitness Institute staff, especially Dr. Berka.

I would also like to thank Bill Gairdner, whose original suggestion was the
inspiration for this book. And finally thanks to my parents for their support
over the years, and to Cheryl and Bryche who make life worth living.

Photograph credits

Manitoba Archives   16, 32
Ontario Ministry of Health   8
Ontario Ministry of Industry and Tourism   42(top), 49
Tourism B.C. Photograph (12663N)   20
Tourism New Brunswick   34

Table of Contents

1/Introduction: Fitness and Health

This is a book on fitness and health for those who have had heart problems, such as cardiac surgery or a heart attack. We hope that this book will be helpful not only to the patient, but to family and friends as well. The central theme is: You, too, can live a healthier, fitter life, starting right now.

I have "been there" and realize that only those who have gone through the process can really know what it is like. Each person is different. My problem: a high cholesterol level resulting in surgery twice within ten years. However, it was also my high level of fitness that helped me to withstand the operations and to recover in a remarkably short period of time. My advice is to have confidence in your doctors, the hospital, and the staff. Take a positive optimistic attitude and you will be the better for it.

Let us start out by taking a look at your heart.

The healthy heart is a very strong organ about the size of your fist, pumping many litres of blood through your blood vessels at an average daily rate of 70 to 80 strokes a minute.

Your heart normally rests twice as long as it works. But during periods of strenuous physical activity or emotional stress, it may beat twice as fast as usual and pump twice as much blood. The faster the heart beats, the harder it works, and the less time it has to rest. However, most hearts can endure great physical exertion without difficulty. Your daily energy, efficiency, and staying power are all limited by the strength of your heart and by your level of physical fitness.

After a few months of regular exercise following your hospital stay, you'll find yourself coping more effectively with physical and emotional stresses. Your mind and body are inseparable — the health of one is bound to affect the health of the other.

Now for some statistics. The Canadian Heart Foundation states that 2 500 000 Canadians of all ages have some form of cardio-vascular ailment. About 35% of these occur among people 45 to 64 years of age.

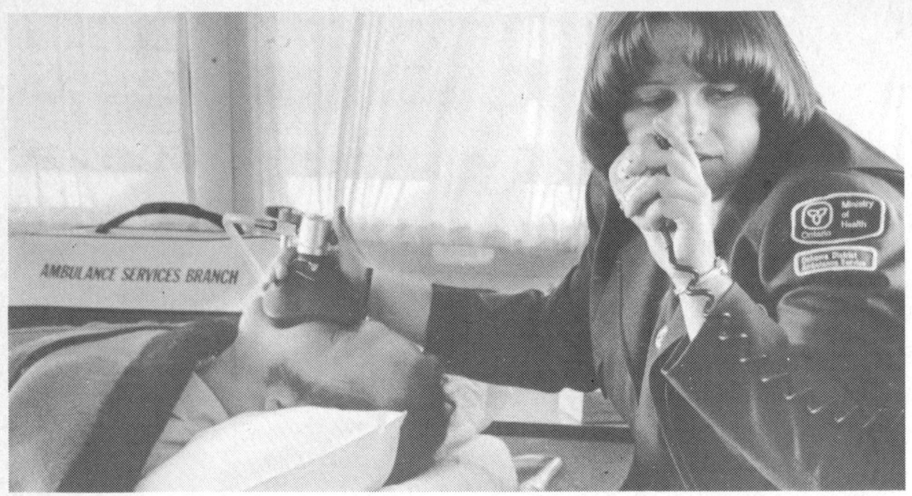

But there is a brighter side because great strides have been made in research, diagnosis, treatment, and control of heart diseases. At present

- Most people who have heart attacks recover.
- High blood pressure (hypertension) can be controlled.
- Rheumatic heart disease can be prevented.
- Most heart defects can be repaired.
- Medical science can do a great deal for people with circulatory disorders.

Now that some of your anxiety has been decreased, let us take a look at what you can do for yourself after the doctors have gone. Your rehabilitation programme may begin during an acute phase of your illness and extend for many months after you have been discharged from hospital. Treatment may include drug therapy, surgery, counselling, education, and exercise. The main purpose is that you can eventually care for yourself and maintain your occupational, recreational, and social activities.

For many, exercise is simply not a priority following hospitalization. In fact, merely getting to the washroom can be a major task. Your exercise programme may start as soon as you are on your feet, or it may be a few days or even weeks before you are able to do anything of a physical nature. Just remember that we each have different problems and a different rate of recovery. The main thing to keep in mind is that, no matter how serious it is, you will be able to do *something* and probably more than you think. Generally speaking, patients can safely start an exercise programme anywhere from three weeks to several months following their illness. The Fitness Institute, for example, usually requires 12 weeks rest after a heart attack and 8 weeks after surgery before prescribing an exercise programme.

One problem most patients find is that they do not receive enough information about exercise before leaving the hospital. Those who start a programme of activity seem to get little encouragement, and often quit after a few weeks. This is a time when the family can provide encouragement; it can be a golden opportunity for *everyone* to start an exercise programme. Having company on your walk will provide the moral support you need to continue.

The intensity of your activity programme depends on the condition you were in prior to entering the hospital or having the heart attack. You will be more frail after your heart attack or surgery. For some of you who have had surgery you will also be more aware of your body. You will start to magnify aches and pains out of proportion. Try to be more sensitive to what your body is "telling you" so that you can distinguish real pain from every-day, run-of-the-mill aches and discomfort.

Today we see millions of people throughout the world taking part in daily routines of exercise. Such positive "lifestyle modification" is not restricted to those who are considered healthy. Today's cardiac patient can often be seen competing in athletic events, even running marathons. But this book is *not a training manual* for cardiac athletes. We are going to talk about fitness, diet, stress-reducing techniques, and we shall provide you with guidelines for not only a home, but also a hospital fitness programme. Who knows? You may even achieve a higher degree of physical fitness than you had, prior to hospitalization.

Finally, always check with your doctors before entering any kind of programme: they will know your condition better than anyone. Your ability to cope with life's daily stresses, and also to manage your health, will improve as you enjoy a fitter, more vigorous lifestyle.

GO FOR IT!

2/The Problem

The causes of cardiac problems are many. Heredity, diet, stress, smoking, and cholesterol, combined with lack of exercise, are the major risk factors leading to heart disease. It is not a simple disease, nor is there a simple guaranteed remedy. In fact, I was competing in road races just prior to surgery and undoubtedly, if I hadn't been physically fit, I would not be here to write this book.

You will find many pitfalls that lie along your path to recovery and ideal fitness. One of the biggest stumbling blocks to taking on a physical fitness programme, is FEAR. You feel violated. You may even deny the illness. Your family will have a misconception of your health; you are worried that your employer will see restrictions in your ability to return to work. These things may give you a lack of confidence and, yes, you may even feel sorry for yourself. These are natural feelings. Do not deny them, acknowledge them and realize that you will overcome them as you progress to fitness.

There are also many other problems related to lack of physical activity which have a bearing on those with cardiac problems, namely:

1. **Decreased Circulation**
   A lack of muscle action (lack of exercise) causes blood circulation to slow down, decreasing the supply of oxygen to the brain, organs, and muscles. An exercise programme will assist you in achieving a lowered resting heart rate, increase the oxygen-carrying capacity of the blood, decrease the level of cholesterol in the blood, and (in some people) lower high blood pressure.

2. **Obesity**
   Lack of exercise can contribute to obesity by a slow, almost unnoticed gain of excess weight caused by lowered use of kilojoules (formerly called calories). (*See Chapter 10 on Nutrition.*)

If you become overweight, you will find daily activity more
difficult, and, most important of all, that extra weight will
place added strain on your heart.

3. Inefficient Heart Muscle

The heart is a muscle and, like any other muscle in your
body, if it isn't exercised properly, it won't do the job well. A
well-exercised heart pumps more blood with each beat than a
''non-exercised heart'' and can be twice as efficient.

4. Poor Posture

As muscles grow lax and give in to the pull of gravity, the
body sags and begins to slump into a very inefficient and
unattractive posture. As you get used to the slump, it feels
natural, so you slump more, and so on. Eventually, the
muscular and tendonous structures of the body adapt to poor
posture, making it permanent.

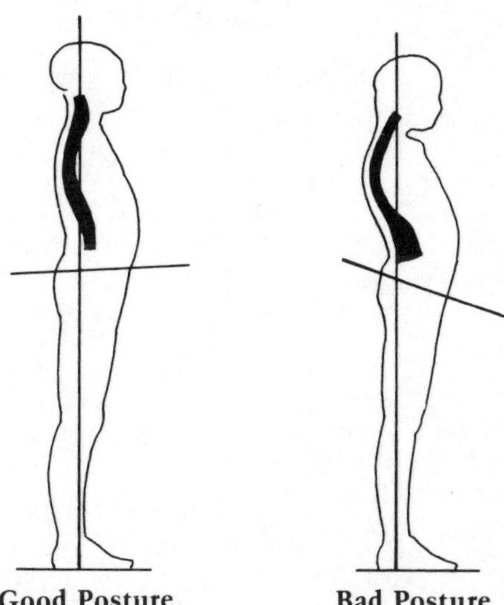

5. Muscular Weakness

Unexercised muscles rapidly grow weak, losing not only
strength but size. Slack muscles also have poor blood flow,
are easily injured, and, because they don't contract very often
or with sufficient strength, the heart and lungs lose this
muscular assistance in returning the blood to be recharged
with oxygen.

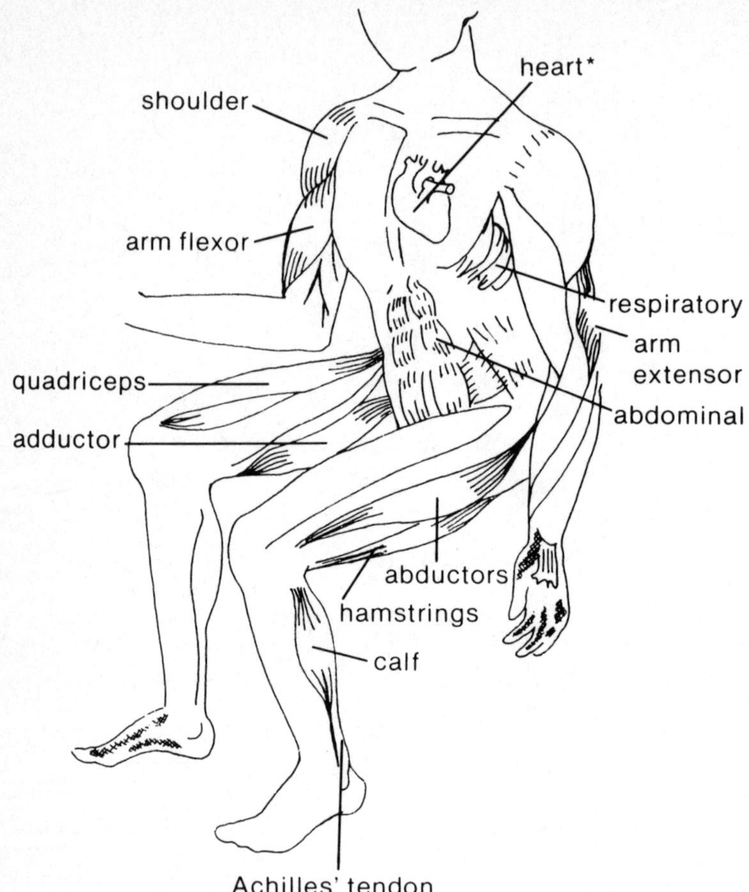

*Although essentially an organ, the heart is actually composed of a very specialized type of muscle tissue.

6. Fatigue

Without enough daily exercise, a feeling of fatigue develops, and fairly easy tasks seem to require greater effort, so we stop doing them . . . doing them . . . doing them.

7. Lowered Self-esteem

The less fit you are, the less able you are to physically control your environment, and the easier it is to view yourself as the victim, rather than the master of your environment. Exercise promotes a sense of accomplishment, well-being, vigour, and control.

3/Know Your Heart

Basically, there are four heart responses that concern you:

1. Resting heart rate;
2. Exercise heart rate;
3. Maximum heart rate;
4. Recovery heart rate.

1. How to Take Your Own Pulse

First you must learn to take your own pulse rate. Using your first three fingers, place them on the carotid artery (see diagram). Now, count the number of heartbeats you feel for six seconds. Add a 0 to that number. That resulting number represents your heart rate per minute. (You may also count your pulse for 10 s, then multiply that number by 6.)

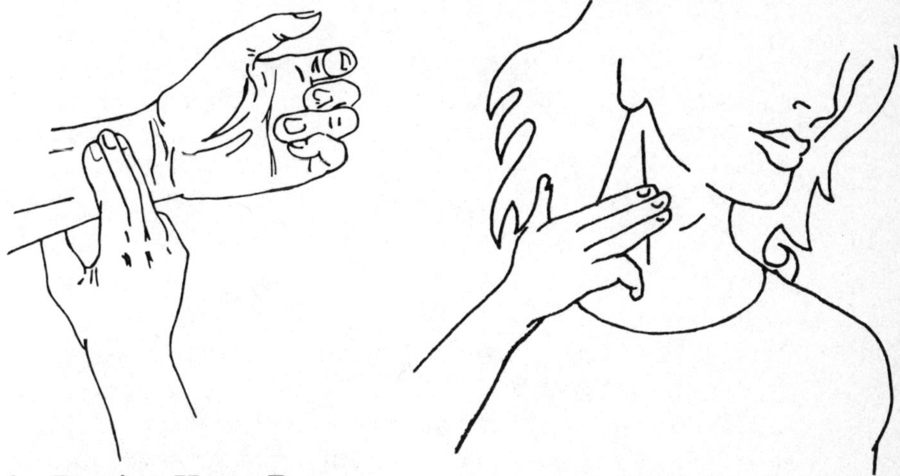

2. Resting Heart Rate

Take your resting heart rate when you are relaxed and resting in your chair. Following hospitalization, your resting pulse rate will be higher than normal. Don't be surprised if your resting rate actually becomes lower in the first few months after you begin a regular exercise programme.

Be sure to monitor your resting pulse on a daily basis, as this will provide you with the base figure needed when you start to exercise.

Why is a Low Resting Heart Rate Desirable?
A low resting heart rate means that your heart doesn't work
as hard to pump blood to your muscles for a given work load,
or effort. A fit heart pumps more blood with each beat, so it
doesn't have to beat as often as an unfit heart. If you could
drop the number of heart beats needed every minute by 10,
through exercise, you could save 14 000 heart beats per day.

3. Exercise Heart Rate

A more detailed description of heart rate during the post-
infarction period will be discussed under the specific chapter
on the fitness programme.

To determine what exercise heart rate you should maintain,
you first need to take a medically supervised exercise test
which is generally associated with cardiac rehabilitation. It
can also be used to test the physiological status of partici-
pants in an adult fitness programme or even to develop
conditioning programmes for athletes.

In your case it will:
  • help in the diagnosis of heart disease;
  • determine your functional cardio-vascular capacity;
  • determine just how much physical activity you can
    do.
  • motivate you to exercise; and
  • evaluate the effects of that exercise programme.

Furthermore, such a test allows a target exercise heart rate to
be determined. Your ability to measure pulse rate before,
during, and after exercise will allow you to know if you
should increase or decrease the intensity of your activity.
Exercise tests can be administered using many different
devices. The most popular are: stepping up and down from a
step; walking on a treadmill; or riding a stationary bicycle.
The use of these standardized methods allows you to
compare results between tests. For the unconditioned cardiac
patient, the test does not usually exceed 14 min.

When the test is being administered, the doctor will usually
monitor the work load, heart rate, blood pressure, and
electrocardiogram. The doctor will be looking for such
symptoms as fatigue, shortness of breath, chest discomfort,
and pain in the legs caused by poor blood circulation.

4. Maximum Heart Rate

This refers to the maximum rate per minute that your heart can beat, and is determined by an exercise stress test. You should never exercise to the extent that your heart is beating at its maximum rate. This could be very dangerous.

5. Recovery Heart Rate

This rate refers to how quickly your heart recovers from intense exercise, and is greatly dependent on your level of physical fitness. The faster your heart rate returns to normal after physical effort, the better your level of fitness. Take your pulse immediately, at two-, four-, and eight-minute intervals after the cardio-respiratory exercise section of your programme. Keep a record of these figures. After a while, this will become one of the best guidelines to your level of endurance fitness.

4/Psychological Factors

One of the primary factors influencing recovery is that of your psychological or mental preparation. Some of the key anxiety-producing factors include:

1. fears arising from hospital treatment;
2. fear of another attack;
3. fear of death;
4. fear of financial distress;
5. fear of inadequacy at work;
6. fear of being unemployed;
7. failure to plan for convalescence and rehabilitation;
8. failure to receive emotional support from the spouse and family.

Prior to hospitalization, you probably experienced pain in the chest, as well as shortness of breath, which limited your physical activity. Following an operation, the bed rest will have further depressed your level of fitness so that a deconditioned state is unavoidable. Therefore, don't be surprised if you experience a loss of strength, flexibility, and endurance, as in all parts of your body you will feel a general body weakness. In short, you may feel as if you're just falling apart. I did.

1. **Confidence**

   As you improve physically you will find that your confidence
   will also take an upturn. Just increasing that short walk
   down the hospital corridor to a turn around the ward will
   give you something to brag about to your visitors.

2. **Anxiety**

   Anxiety is at its strongest on Day One; this is caused by fear
   of what has happened and the body's response to the event.
   By the second day your anxiety begins to lessen dramatically
   and you may now begin to deny that anything happened. On
   Day Three, depression may take over, with a growing awareness of what has really happened, and the consequences of
   the event on your life. This depression may continue for two
   to three days, but in most cases by Day Five or Six, you will
   begin to resume your usual personality and emotional
   pattern. If you find that after six days you are still depressed,
   then ask for help in the form of counselling.

   One method to ease your mind and reduce anxiety is to ask
   the nurse to explain the purpose and activities of all the
   monitors that pertain to your care. Explanation of the activities and therapies in the coronary care unit can be the first
   step in your education programme. You may find, at this
   time, that your ability to absorb information will be limited,
   so write down things as they are explained to you. Be sure
   that all the basic elements such as exercise, diet, medication,
   sexual activity, and cardiac symptoms are explained. It
   would be a good idea to have your spouse, partner, or a friend
   in attendance when this explanation takes place, as they will
   remember many of the things that you, in your anxiety, may
   forget. Also ask for more detailed explanation when the
   doctor, nurse, or physiotherapist says "Do it in moderation"
   or "Use your own discretion." Ask for specific written and
   verbal direction as to what you are supposed to do.

3. **Return to Work**

   Returning to work is a great psychological boost for those
   who have experienced cardiac problems. Research has shown
   that a majority of patients can return to work on a full or
   limited basis. With your physician's help, evaluate the
   energy cost of doing your job. When you make this appraisal,

take into consideration not only the work that you have to
do, but the physical cost of getting to work (i.e., dressing,
shaving, driving your car, and walking to the job). Finally,
you should know that emotional stress can be as taxing as
physical work. Your body, under great emotional stress, may
be performing the work of a white collar worker, while your
heart is doing the work of a person shovelling coal in a steel
mill.

Many household tasks take as much energy as an average job
in industry. Evaluation of all tasks should be undertaken
prior to assuming the duties.

A functional exercise test will provide you with the bench
marks needed when appraising your ability to return to work.

4. Lifestyle

As your feeling of well-being increases and you begin to
return to many of your normal daily activities, it is important that you take time to evaluate your previous lifestyle
and determine what changes need to be made.

One change is to eliminate as much stress as possible from
your life. Did you know that stress is one of the major causes

for over two thirds of the visits to family doctors? Some questions that you can ask yourself are:

- How stressful was my life prior to my illness?
- What are the things that made my life stressful?
- How really serious are they? Am I taking everything too seriously?
- What are the things that can be eliminated so that I will not aggravate my present condition?

Your first challenge will be to know the symptoms of increased stress; such things as an increase in heart rate, blood pressure, bladder pressure, and stomach acidity are signs that you may be pushing yourself too much.

Try to predict when stressful situations may occur and then try to deal with them. Face stress with a positive attitude, don't make unreasonable demands on yourself. Try to distinguish between what is important and what is not. Include such activities as meditation, biofeedback, and scientific relaxation to help you lower your anxiety level. Coping strategies include removing the stressful situation, scaling down your expectations, developing and using your family and social support system, changing activities, planning rest periods, and above all — having fun.

5. A Defence System

A number of suggestions have been made to help you improve your defence system against further difficulties and to provide you with a strategy for minimizing anxiety. These do work, but there is one problem and that's what we call the ''New Year's Resolution'' solution. It is no solution at all. Humans don't change that quickly, no matter how serious the crisis has been. When learning a new strategy, you will go through the usual process. According to Dr. Harold Minden of York University's Psychology Department, this process includes four stages:

1. the awkward, discomfort stage;
2. the comfortable, satisfied-it's-getting-better stage;
3. the mature stage; and
4. the you-have-arrived stage.

You will do a lot of selective forgetting as time goes on and that is part of the healing process. Don't forget those good intentions and promises that you made, such as to exercise and watch your diet, as well as getting plenty of rest. In the beginning, it may hurt; it may be difficult; but I promise you that it will get better if you stay at it.

Finally, an area of great misinformation is that concerning sexual activity following a heart attack, cardiac surgery, or hospitalization. Although sexual activity produces a heart rate between 97 and 117 beats per minute, which is an energy level equal to climbing two flights of stairs, the best advice is to take your time and not be so athletic as you once might have been. You may even find a slower pace will provide increased satisfaction.

5/Hospital Fitness Programme

There are two kinds of hospital rehabilitation programme, one
for those who have experienced a heart attack, the other for
cardiac surgery patients. The following activities should be
attempted only if approved by your doctor or therapist.

The patient who has undergone uncomplicated coronary artery
bypass surgery can begin with some light activity during the first
day following the operation, while still in the intensive care
unit. On the first day in the intensive care unit, low levels of
activity can include such things as partial self-care (washing
hands and face, brushing teeth), simple active-passive arm and
leg movements, and the bending and stretching of the ankles
several times a day.

By the second day, you may be feeding yourself a soft diet,
somewhat shakily, and may be assisted out of bed to a chair. At
the time of transfer out of the intensive care unit, which is
usually on or after the second day, you may have walked with
the help of the nurse.

Once you have been released from the intensive care unit, the
object is to develop a routine for your exercise programme. Your
object is to be able to perform complete self-care by the time you
are discharged from the hospital. In general, low-intensity calisthenics and exercises that maintain muscle tone, coordination,
and joint mobility are recommended.

At each stage of progress, the level of your activity should be
that which can be performed without discomfort or abnormal
responses. Some discomfort in the chest and leg area is unavoidable. Things to look for are shortness of breath, pain in the
chest, a heart rate greater than 120 beats per minute, or fatigue.

If possible, you should sit in a chair for your meals, get in and
out of bed frequently. Standing up (straight) and walking with
assistance is encouraged. Casual, but routine walks with a nurse
will supplement your calisthenics. A walking programme is next
initiated in the hospital corridors, with the distance and the pace

progressively increased. Assistance in walking is usually required from the third to the fifth post-operative day. After that time, you should feel stable enough to walk alone, or with a family member. By the sixth day, the average patient is usually able to walk alone. At this point you can establish a habit of regular exercise that will stay with you when you leave the hospital. Take your walks at nearly the same time each day, increasing the time and distance that you travel.

The following simple exercises may be used to supplement your walking programme: Be sure to breathe while exercising; *"Do not hold your breath"*; and *"Do not squeeze the chest area."*

1. **Bed Exercise**
   The first group of exercises can be done in bed and should be started as soon as possible.
   Bring knee up to chest, lower leg slowly to a count of 20. Repeat with each leg 20 times. Do not straighten legs.

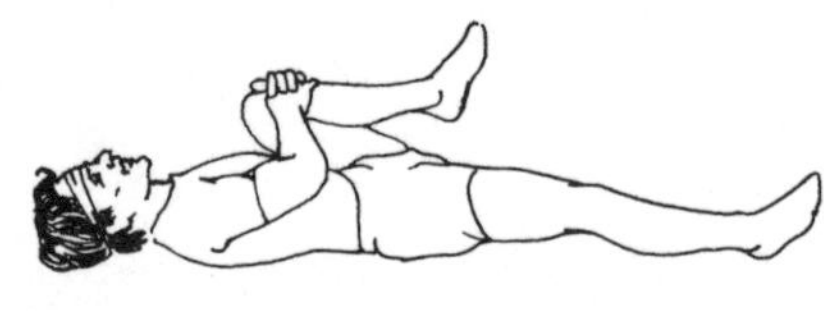

2. **Ankle Rotation**
   Lying or sitting in bed, rotate each foot in a circle first to the left, then to the right. Start with 20 circles in each direction, adding 5 rotations each day to a maximum of 50.

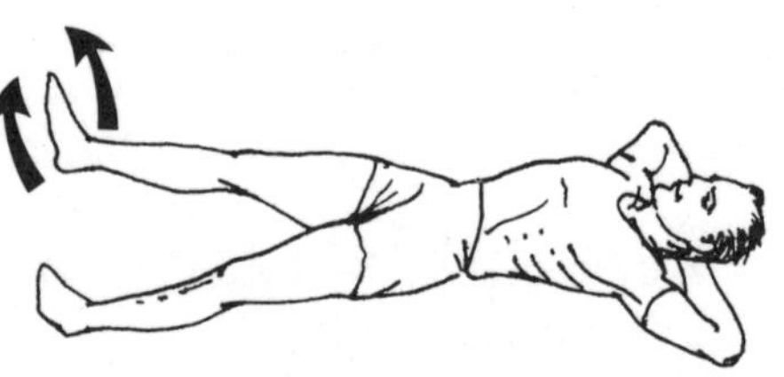

3. **Shoulder Shrugs**
   Sitting in a chair or on the bed, lift your shoulders up trying to touch your ears. Do this 10 times adding two shrugs at each session until you have reached 50 shrugs.

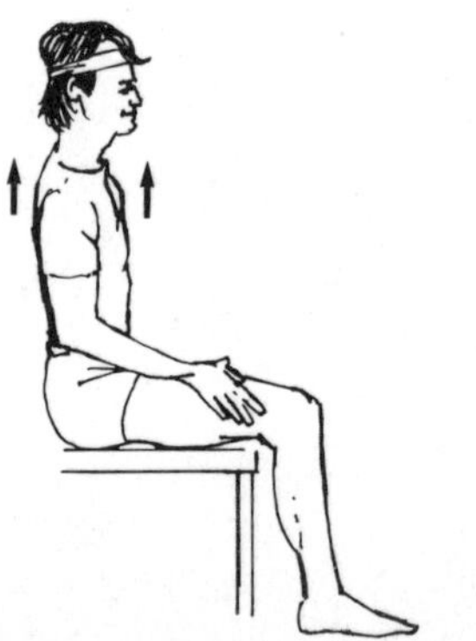

4. Stomach Tightening

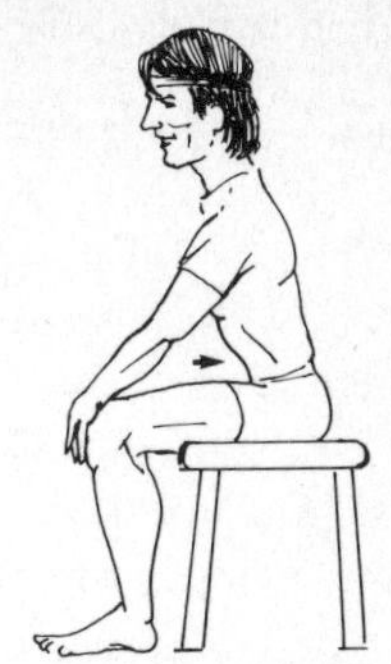

Sit on a chair with your feet flat on the floor and spaced shoulder width apart. Rest your hands lightly on your knees.

Begin the exercise by pulling your stomach in as far as you can and then letting it relax completely. Pull in as far as possible each time and continue until you have done 10 repetitions. Add two repetitions every other workout until you are doing a total of 25. Coordinate your breathing so that you exhale as you pull your abdomen in and inhale as you let it relax.

5. Body Turns

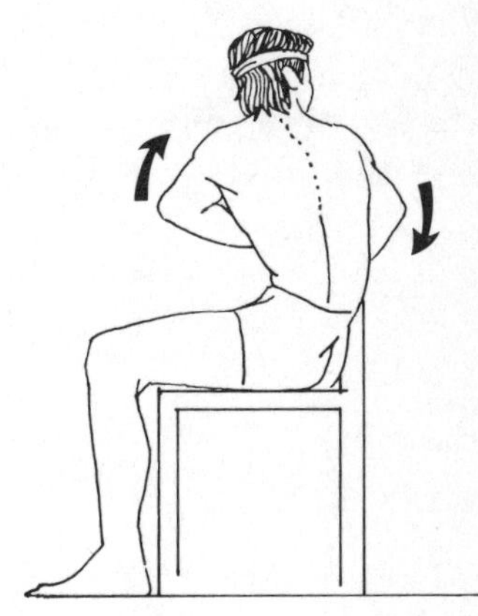

Sitting in a chair, twist the upper body so that you are looking over your shoulder. Alternate to the left and right.

Start with three turns in each direction, adding two turns every second time you exercise.

6. Upper Body Twist

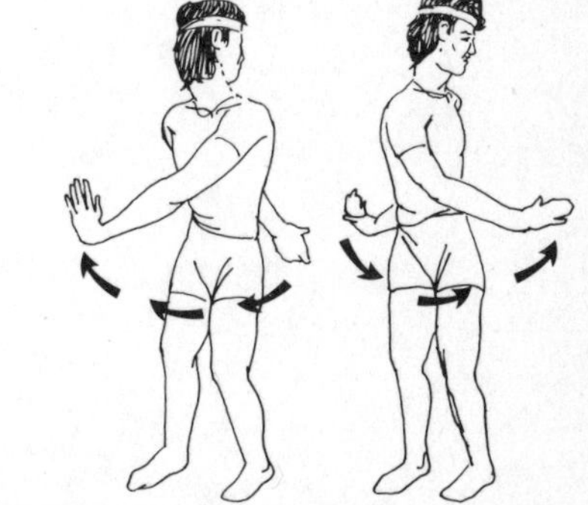

This exercise will promote improvement in the flexibility of the upper body muscles. Stand with your arms hanging relaxed at your sides, feet spaced shoulder width apart.

Begin the exercise by turning your upper body as far to the right as possible, letting the arms swing loosely in the same direction. Your head should also turn in the direction of the swing. Next reverse the procedure and turn as far as possible in the opposite direction.

Continue at an even, moderate pace until you have done a total of 30 turns, 15 to each side. Add two repetitions every other workout until you are doing a total of 50 turns, 25 to each side.

7. Half Squat

This exercise will tone and strengthen the upper leg muscles as well as improve your cardio-respiratory conditioning. Stand with feet about shoulder width apart, toes pointing straight ahead; keep heels flat on the floor through the exercise. Bend your knees and squat down until the upper part of your legs are parallel to the floor, hips at knee level.  Keep your back straight and the upper body as upright as possible. Rise immediately, breathing out as you return to the standing position. Complete eight repetitions, then rest for 30 s before doing eight more repetitions. Add two repetitions every other workout until you reach 14, then go back to eight repetitions, repeating three times.

8. Trunk Bending

Alternate bending slightly forward, backward, and sideways. Do not lean too far in each direction until you have been discharged from the hospital. Start by repeating each movement three times. Repeat each set of exercises three times with a 20-s rest in between. Add 2 repetitions of each exercise every other workout until you reach a maximum of 20. 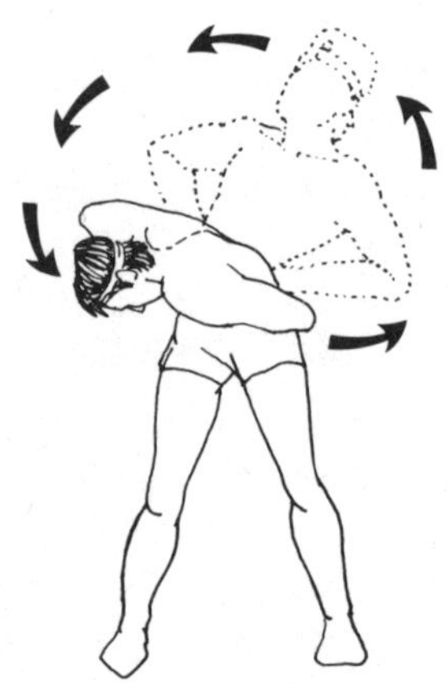

9. Stretching Exercises

If you find that because of lack of conditioning your muscles lack the ability to stretch, you may wish to try the basic leg stretching while sitting in the bath tub as shown. Exhale when bending forward — don't hold your breath during any of the stretching exercises.

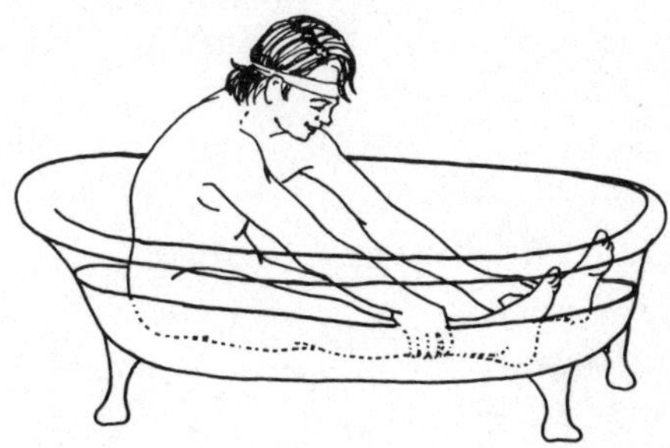

The following stretching exercises can be done while sitting in bed. Note that, when stretching, you do the exercise until you begin to feel a slight discomfort in the muscle area being stretched. Hold the position for 20 s, then repeat three times.

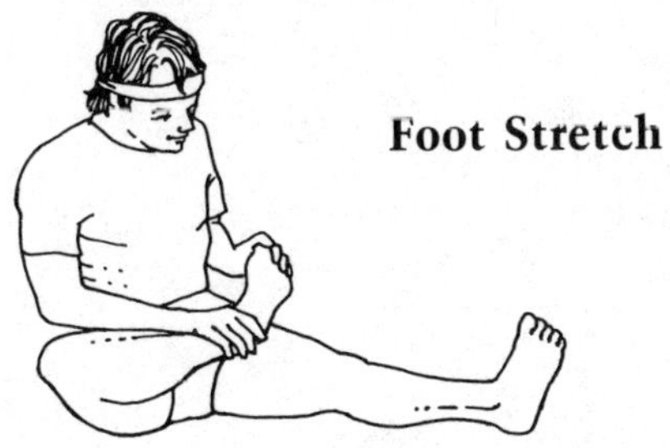

Foot Stretch

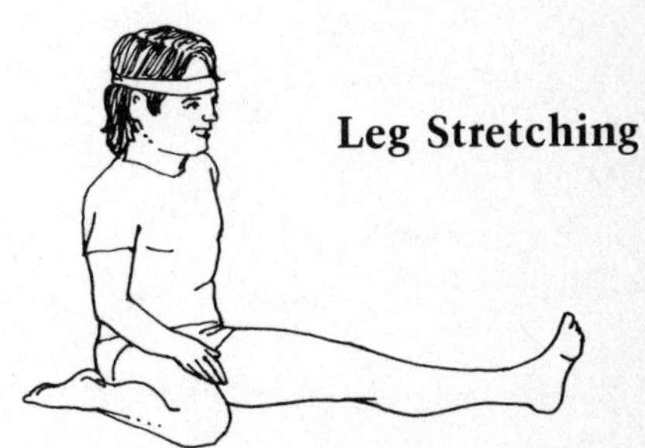

Leg Stretching

Depending on your condition, you may find these exercises too easy or too difficult. Let your body be your guide, as you add or subtract the number of repetitions and sets that you perform. Slow and easy will pay off.

6/Home Fitness Test

Although your physical fitness, in a "total" sense, involves many qualities, its chief requirements are:

1. Cardio-respiratory (heart-lung) efficiency;
2. Muscular and joint flexibility;
3. Freedom from excess fat.

We call all of these true "fitness" factors, because they can be changed, whereas height, for example, can't be changed. There are no widely accepted standards available for the cardiac patient. Regardless of this fact, there is no reason why you can't record your own level of fitness, as well as your rate of improvement through a home fitness programme.

Note: *Be sure to receive clearance from your physician before you undergo any fitness test or programme.*

The following simple tests will give you a good indication of how you rate in the four areas listed above. Try them when you are feeling rested and relaxed. Don't smoke, eat, drink coffee or tea, exercise, or do anything strenuous the day before your test. Ask a friend to assist you with the test. The only equipment you'll need is a pencil and paper to record your findings and a watch with a second hand.

1. Cardio-Respiratory Efficiency

Note: *This area of assessment should not be done on your own until your physician says that it is within your ability.*

Scientifically monitored stress tests are the only sure way of determining your cardio-respiratory efficiency, from which a proper exercise work load can be prescribed. However, monitoring of your own heart over specific distances and times can be used to measure improvement.

The establishment of a base rate is most important. Select a distance that you can comfortably walk in 10-min. Take your pulse at the beginning, after five minutes, and at the end of the walk.

There is still no way to compare your heart's response to the above ''test'' with other cardiac patients. But don't let this discourage you; by becoming familiar with how your heart responds to effort, you will be able to monitor your future improvement. This is possible by simply measuring the distance you travelled during the 10-min walk (using a 400-m track for this test is the easiest). Then, in the future, as a means of re-testing your improved fitness, you simply walk for 10 min, noting the distance covered and your heart rate at the three intervals. If you cover the same amount of distance, but with a lower heart rate, you've improved. If you cover more distance, and your heart rate is the same, or lower than the original test, you've also improved.

Don't forget, lack of sleep, emotional stress, medication, fatigue, or caffeine can alter (usually speed up) your heart rate. So be well rested before a test effort.

2. Muscular and Joint Flexibility

Remember that you can't compare your flexibility to that of others. The important thing is where you start and where you finish. You can test lower-body flexibility by sitting on the floor and trying to outreach your toes with your legs straight out in front of you (see diagram). If you cannot reach your toes, then you need more body flexibility. By improving this factor, you reduce the risk of lower-back injury and hamstring pulls.

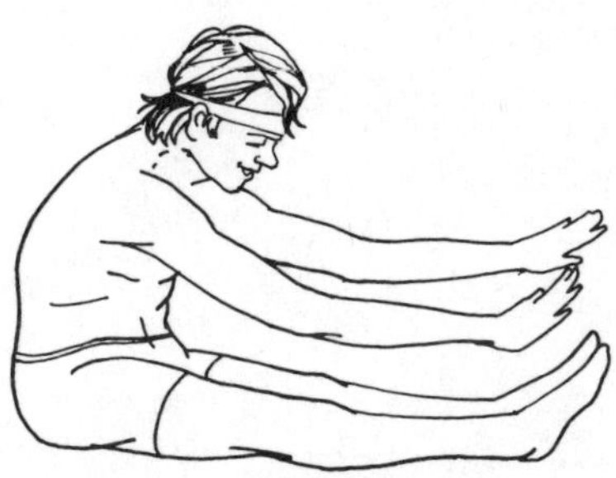

To test your shoulder flexibility, place your hands on your hips with your index fingers on your hip bones. Now, squeeze your elbows together behind your back and have someone measure the distance between them. This is also an ideal way to test how your incision is doing, if you've had open-heart surgery.

3. Freedom from Excess Fat

The "pinch-test" is a simple means of determining how much excess fat you are carrying. Sitting in a relaxed position, in your underclothes or light attire, see how much skin and underlying fat you can pinch between your thumb and forefinger. For men test the back of the upper arm, or 2.5 cm (1 inch) below the shoulder blade. For women test the triceps midway between the shoulder and elbow. (Fold should be taken with the elbow and wrist bent at 90°), or one centimetre above the point of the iliac crest (hip). Tighten the underlying muscles first, so you pinch up only skin and fat. The thickness of the skinfold will tell the story. If you are not sure of the above, have your doctor or fitness leader show you how at your next check-up.

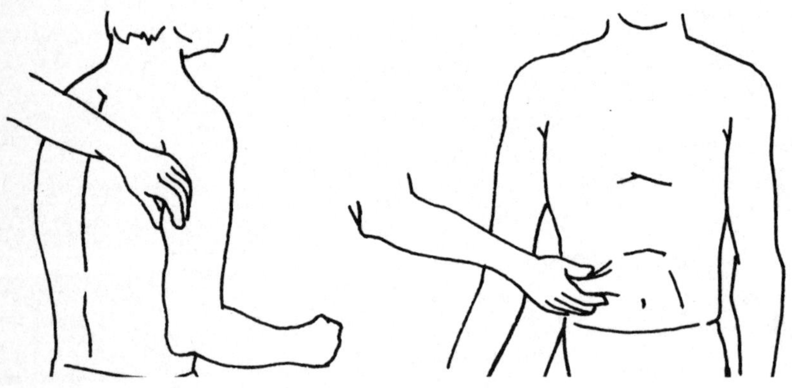

Skinfold thickness*		Rating
7 mm or less	(0-1/4")	Excellent
8-13 mm	(1/4"-1/2")	Good
14-18 mm	(1/2"-3/4")	Fair
19-25 mm	(3/4"-1")	Poor
26 mm or more	(1" or more)	Very Poor

* Imperial units are included in this chart for adults who were not in school when metric measurement was introduced.

Just a reminder, your absolute body weight is not the important factor, it's the breakdown between fat and non-fat weight. It is the amount of fat over and above normal that is the risk factor, not simply body weight. Therefore, it is important that you have body-fat content monitored closely.

Recording Your Test Results

Now that you have completed the Home Fitness Test, it's important to record the results, so that you can chart your progress for the future. The following is a model of a recording chart. Copy this chart, and simply fill in the relevant data for each section. Don't forget to record the date of each test. You should retest yourself every two months in order to gauge improvement.

HOME FITNESS TEST RESULTS

1. 10-Min walk

	Test 1	Test II	Test III	Comments
Date:				
Resting heart rate:				
5-min heart rate:				
Distance covered:				
Exercise rate:				
Recovery heart rate: (taken 1 min after walk)				

2. Muscle and Joint Flexibility

Date:			
Toe touch			
Elbow touch			

3. Body Fat

Date:			
Shoulder blade (men)			
Triceps (women)			

Fitness Institute
Cardiac Rehabilitation Programme
DAILY RECORD

Name ____

Date	Exercise	Distance	Time	Resting Heart Rate	
Example	Walking	800 m	10 min	75	

Heart Rate 5 min	Heart Rate 10 min	Heart Rate 15 min	Heart Rate 2 min after exercise	Heart Rate 4 min after exercise	Heart Rate 8 min after exercise
90	100	105	100	95	90

The Ten Commandments of Fitness

Throughout your fitness programme don't forget the Ten Commandments of Fitness:

1. TRAIN, DON'T STRAIN: Fitness can be fun. Learn to work hard without suffering. Be sure you have medical clearance from your physician. We strongly recommend a fitness test each time you move to a higher level of work intensity.

2. WARM UP AND COOL DOWN GRADUALLY: This applies to all physical activity.

3. LEARN YOUR TRAINING HEART RATE: Always know how much physical stress you can place on your heart. Know when to slow down or speed up.

4. BE PHYSICALLY ACTIVE DAILY: Once you have recovered from your surgery or heart attack, begin a regular exercise programme.

5. BREATHE RYTHMICALLY, WITH BODY MOVEMENT: Do not perform any breath-holding or isometric-type exercises, breathe normally and naturally while exercising.

6. STRETCH SLOWLY: Don't bounce. Static stretching reduces injuries and is more effective.

7. LESS IS BEST: It is far better to underdo it than to overdo it. However, in the long run, expect to be able to do more than when you began your exercise programme.

8. PRACTISE RELAXATION: This helps reduce tension and leads to more effective exercise performance.

9. EAT WISELY: Good fitness requires good nutrition. Avoid toxic substances such as nicotine, caffeine, and alcohol; and reduce intake of refined sugar, salt, and animal fats. Do not eat or drink at least three hours prior to exercise (small amount of water is permitted).

10. MONITOR: If you notice any unaccustomed symptoms, slow down, or stop and see your doctor.

7/Home Fitness Programme

Rehabilitation, following discharge from the hospital, means a continuation of the exercises initiated in the hospital, with a progressive increase in the number of repetitions performed.

Usually the hospital will provide you with a basic home exercise programme to follow for the first few weeks after your discharge. If you live near the hospital, you may be able to take part in their exercise programme for out-patients. However, as not all patients are able to take advantage of this service, here are some tips on what to do once you are home.

First, follow your doctor's instructions which will probably include walking around your home. If the weather is warm, a short walk out-of-doors will be most beneficial both physically and psychologically. Doesn't the air smell terrific?

Do something every day, even if it's not as much as you had planned on doing. Try to exercise at the same time each day so

that it becomes a habit. If you are a high achiever, don't overdo it. Slow, steady progress is the best way to improve your fitness level.

If the ankle on a leg that donated a vein begins to swell, it does not necessarily mean that you must stop walking. The elevation of the leg on a pillow or the use of an elastic stocking may just solve the problem. Muscle soreness and chest pain should have decreased to the point that you are performing your exercise programme at an increased level of intensity.

Two weeks following surgery, if you have no shortness of breath, no chest discomfort, no irregular beating of the heart, and a good level of tolerance for exercise, then a daily walking programme can be initiated. This can begin with walking at least 800 m (1/2 mile) in 10 min. Take your heart rate prior to, during, and after the exercise. Record it. BE SURE THAT THE NUMBER OF BEATS PER MINUTE IS WITHIN YOUR TARGET ZONE. Learn your training heart rate range. Exercise is most beneficial at your prescribed Training Heart Rate Range (T.H.R.R.). At poor, good, and excellent levels of condition, your T.H.R.R. will be, respectively, about 65%, 75%, and 85% of your Maximum Heart Rate. Initially, cardiac patients should determine their Maximum Heart Rate under the controlled conditions and supervision of a doctor. A great deal has been written about age-adjusted, peak heart-rate levels. Approximately 15% of the cardiac population can reach their peak adjusted heart-rate levels without other abnormality. The remaining 85% will be limited with some abnormality at a heart rate 85% less than the age-predicted, peak heart-rate estimate.

Try to walk in a level area and save the hills for a later time. If this first bout of exercise is handled well, then gradually increase the distance so that you are now walking 1600 m (one mile) in about 20 min then increase the distance so that you are walking up to at least 3200 m (two miles). If there are no complications, you could increase the distance walked at the end of 8 weeks to 4800 m (3 miles) at a speed of 4.8 km (3 miles) per hour. Often the 10% rule is a good one: never try to increase your work load more than 10% per week (i.e., covering about 1.5 km/20 min). If you experience unusual discomfort, or stress, such as chest pain, shortness of breath, or pain in the legs, consult your cardiologist.

Wear loose-fitting clothing, comfortable shoes, and avoid exercising out-of-doors during extreme weather conditions (heat, cold, humidity, or pollution alerts) or immediately following a meal. Do not exercise when ill or overly tired. Pleasant fatigue, a sweat, and becoming slightly flushed is a desirable result of exercise, but exhaustion is not.

There will be a great variation in exercise tolerance among patients, depending on such factors as age, motivation, and the type of heart problem. One method of determining if you can increase your exercise programme is to evaluate your response to a 10% increase of your activity load. If you do not experience discomfort, you can probably move to the next level. The importance of continued monitoring is essential for one wanting to increase the exercise programme. Long, slow distance should be your guide.

Your optimal exercise programme should consist of three distinct phases:

1. **Warm-up:**
   This usually consists of 10 min of light rhythmical calisthenics and stretching exercises. Working with hands above the shoulders is harder on the heart than working with arms below the shoulders. Breathe normally. *"Do not hold your breath."*

2. **Exercise:**
   Consists of walking and eventually jogging, cycling, or swimming, the object being to increase your heart rate to a level recommended by your cardiologist and determined by a functional, graded exercise test.

3. **Cooling down:**
   Should consist of 5-10 min of low-intensity exercise. This helps to lower the heart rate slowly and prevent pooling of blood in the legs, thus avoiding the undesirable effects of abrupt stopping of high-intensity exercise, such as light-headedness or nausea.

At approximately 8-10 weeks after surgery, another exercise stress test should be performed. The results will provide you with guidance in continuing your exercise programme. At this stage, you may wish to join a fitness class designed especially for those undergoing cardiac rehabilitation. Group programmes provide real motivation and can be a lot of fun. You begin to exercise because you enjoy it not because you are afraid. A point to remember about group programmes is that they are usually designed for the average fitness level of the group. You may find the activities too strenuous or too easy for your specific condition, so some adaptation will have to be made by you and the instructor.

During winter months, when it is too cold for walking or jogging out-of-doors, riding a stationary exercise bicycle indoors is an excellent way to maintain your fitness level. The stationary bicycle can usually be ridden within two months of your discharge from the hospital. It is recommended that you start pedalling at about 50 revolutions per minute, adjusting the tension so that you can safely reach your training heart rate. To avoid back problems and muscular fatigue, adjust the seat so that when the leg is extended your heel will fit firmly on the

pedal. Take a couple of turns backwards; if you lose contact
with the pedal, the seat is too high. Relax and use a light comfortable grip on the handle bars. If your heart rate is above your
target level then lower the resistance rather than your pedalling
speed. The bicycle does not place the same level of stress on the
heart as running so that your work load will need to be increased.
MONITOR YOUR HEART RATE AND BE SURE THAT THE NUMBER OF BEATS
PER MINUTE IS WITHIN YOUR TARGET ZONE. Some people say that
riding an exercise bicycle is boring. The following tips will help
you to overcome this problem:

1. Exercise while you listen to the radio — we suggest that a
    newscast may prove to be an appropriate time.
2. Watch your favourite television show. (Don't become so
    involved in the show that you forget to take your pulse.)
3. Read a book or a newspaper during your ride.
4. Exercise at the same time each day, or you may vary your
    schedule, whichever gives you the incentive to continue your
    programme.

For a cardiac patient to maintain a training effect the formal
exercise programme must involve:

1. Reaching a target heart rate as determined through appro-
    priate testing.
2. An exercise session may go to about 60 min in length, and
    include warm-up and cooling-down periods.
3. The frequency should be from three to six times per week.
4. The level of exertion should not be increased until after
    appropriate testing. If exercise has been discontinued for a
    two-week period, you should be re-evaluated and once again
    build up your target level.

Finally, there are really two types of exercise programmes, the
formal, which we have just been discussing, and the informal.
The informal is meant to develop a more active lifestyle, such
as:

— getting off the bus two blocks before your stop and walking to
    your destination.
— leaving the elevator one floor below your destination and
    walking up the stairs.

I'm sure that you can think of many other ways to give yourself the opportunity of becoming physically fit throughout the day.

The following exercises may be used in your warm-up and cool-down period. Your doctor or therapist will also have exercises that you can use during this period.

1. Stretching Exercises

Hold each position for 20 s. Repeat each stretching exercise three times. Stretch slowly. Do not "bounce".

Lying Knee pull to Chest

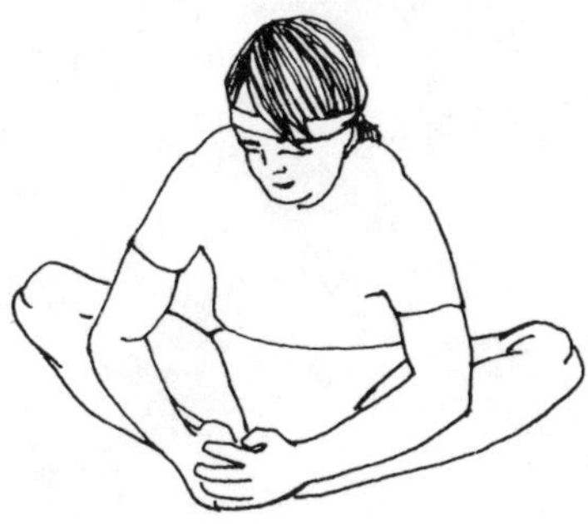

Low Back Stretch

**Quarter
Squats**

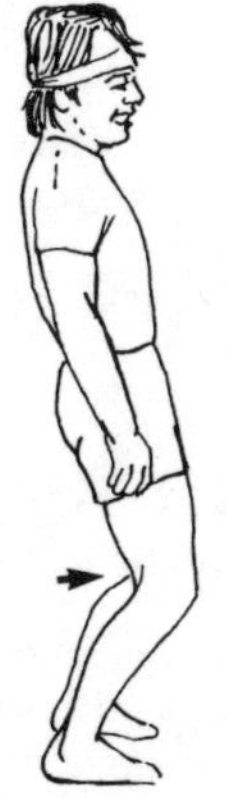

**Back
Thigh pull**

(If back pain
is a problem,
replace with
Seated Double
Leg Stretch)

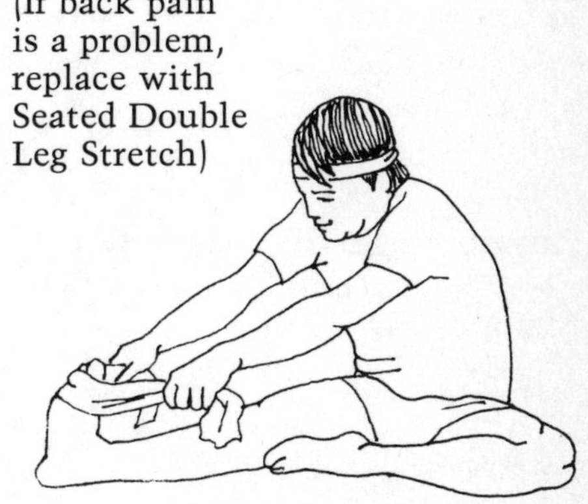

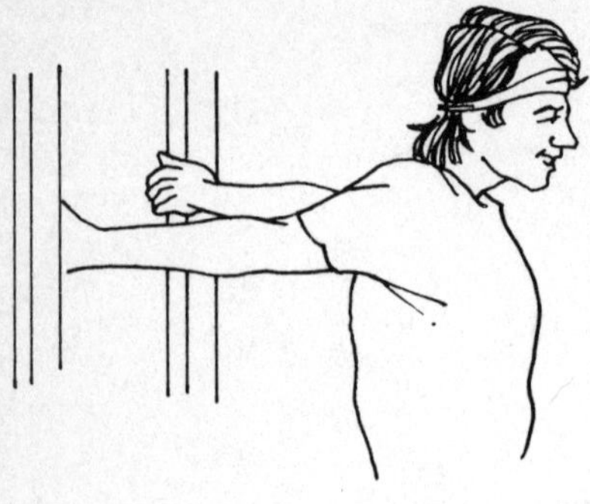

Triceps and
Shoulder Stretch

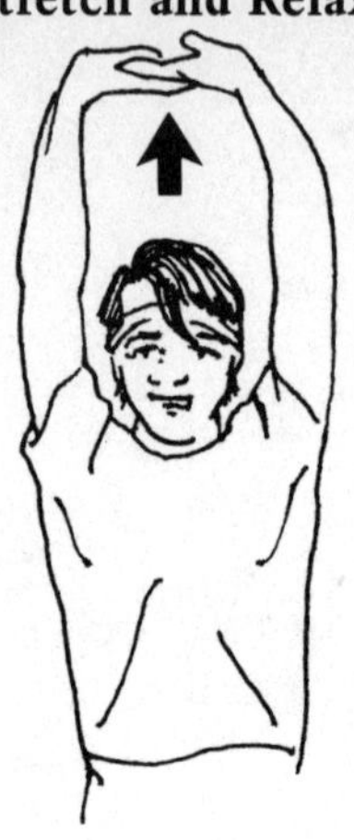

High Stretch and Relax

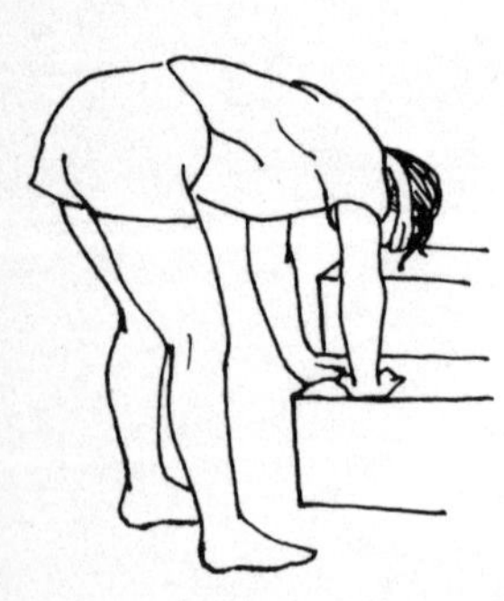

Calf and
Achilles stretch

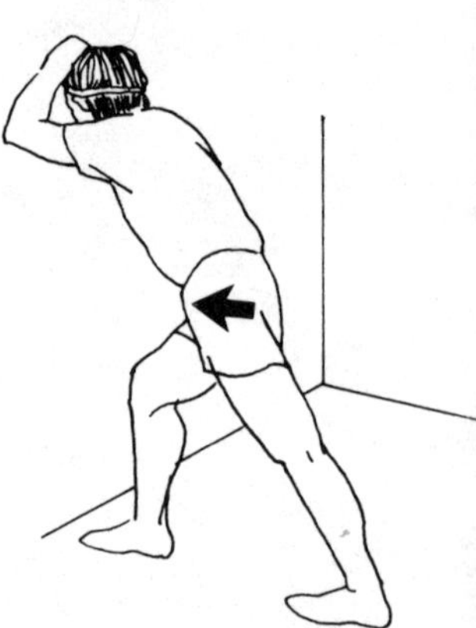

Shoulder
hyperextension

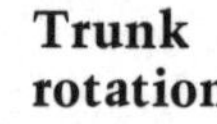

Trunk
rotation

2. Calisthenics

Torso Twist

Arm Drill

Seated Knee Lift - Head Touch

3. Trunk Rotation

Starting Position

One

Two

Three

Four

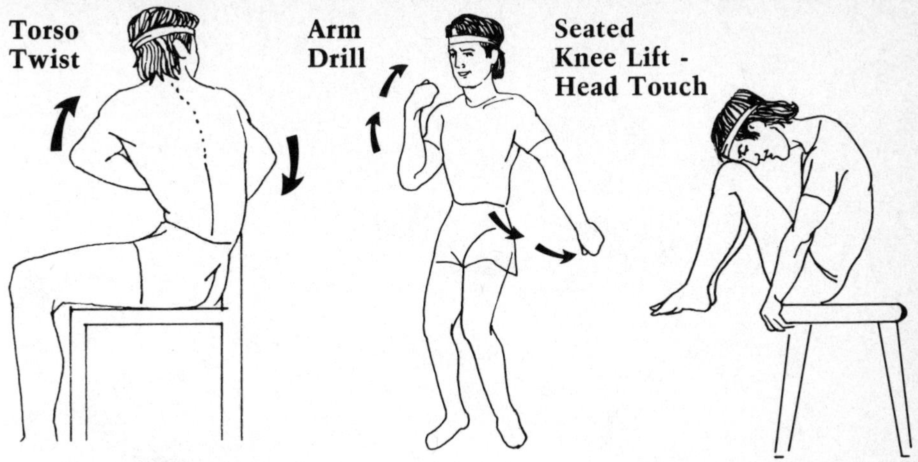

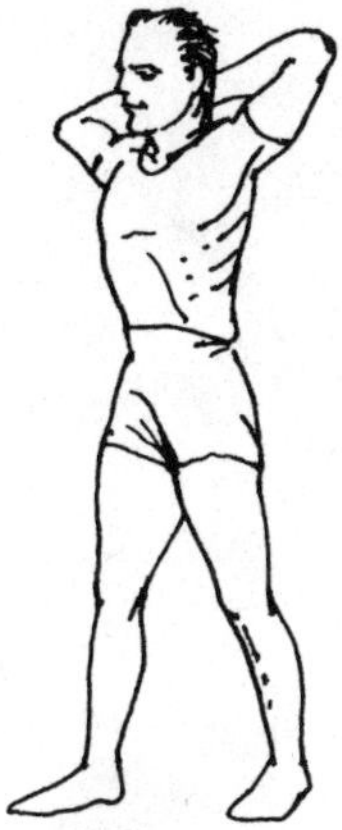

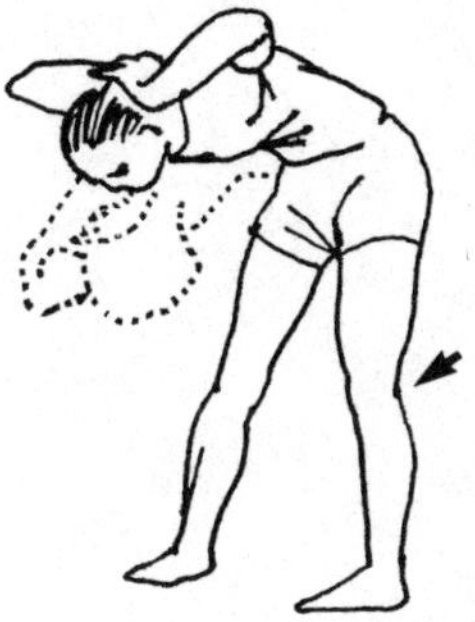

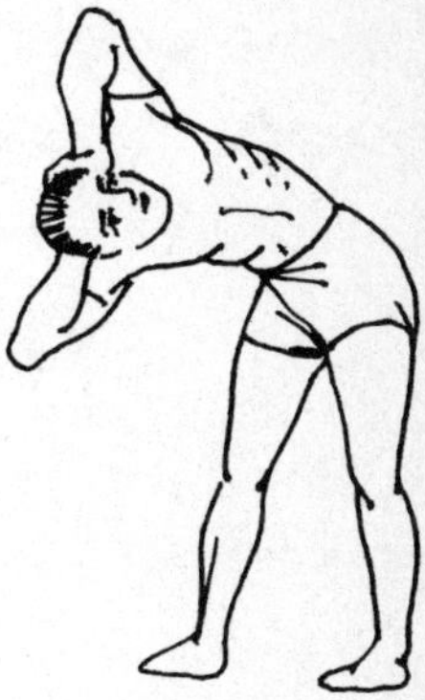

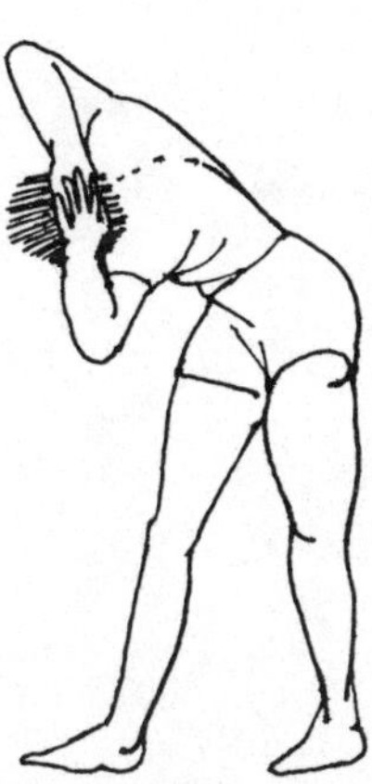

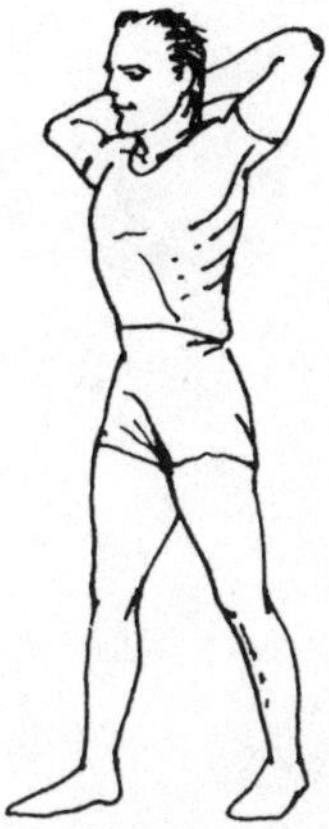

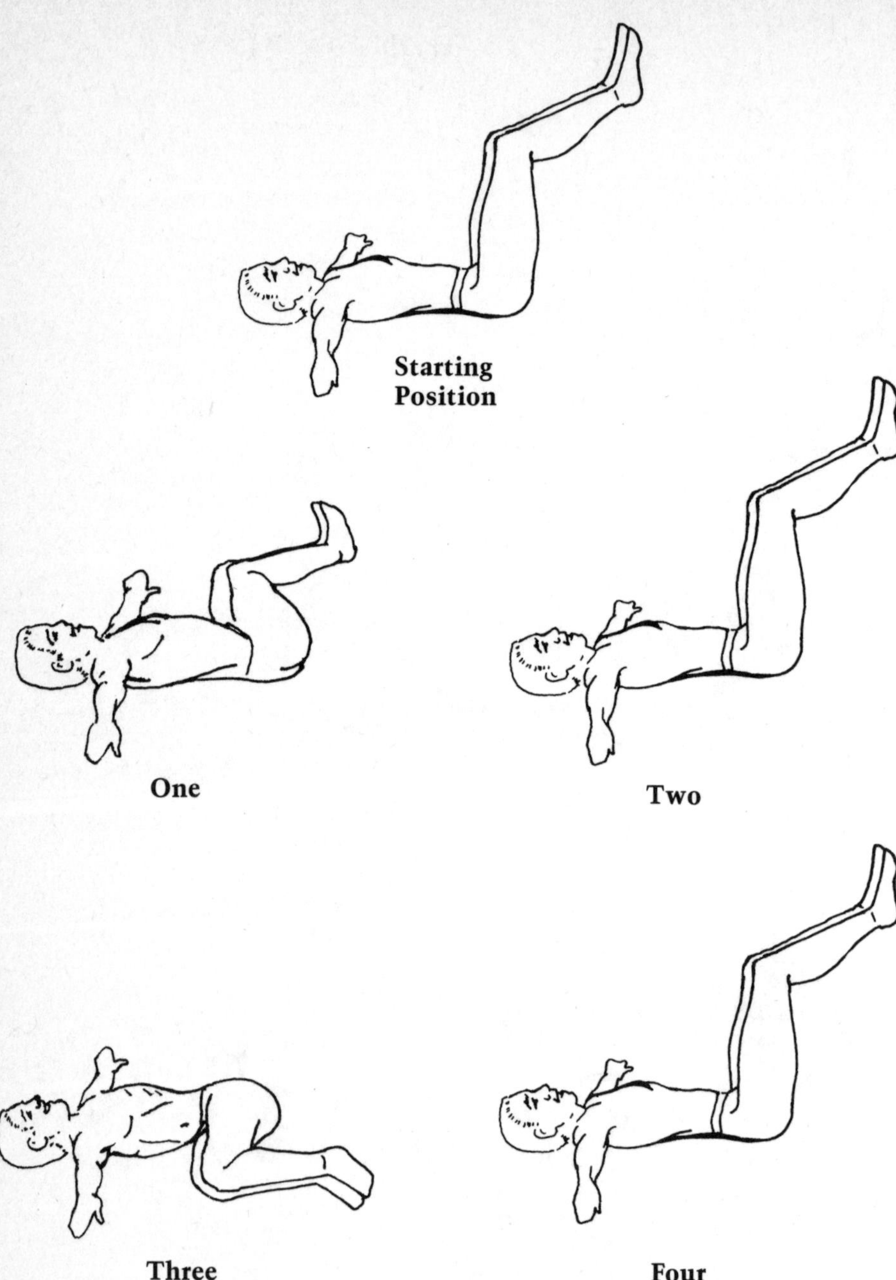

Starting
Position
One
Two
Three
Four

8/Stress — How to Relieve It

Stress is a universal problem in today's society. In response to stress, our muscles contract involuntarily, creating knots of tension. You may experience this tension when preparing for an exam, trying out for a team, or in your dealings with your boss. The tightened muscles squeeze blood vessels and reduce circulation, which may lead to headaches, dizzy spells, painful muscle spasms, and fatigue. The most effective *natural* antidote for stress is physical exercise. Physical activity also helps get rid of the excess adrenalin and fats which accumulate in the blood stream when you are under stress. The following techniques are effective stress reducers.

1. Deep Breathing

One of the most widely used techniques for inducing relaxation is simple deep breathing. By developing the skills of deep breathing (diaphragmatic breathing) and complete expansion of the lungs, you will obtain optimal oxygen intake and, in turn, carbon dioxide waste will be properly expelled from your lungs. Diaphragmatic breathing is not learned without practice. Once learned, however, the technique can be practised anywhere, anytime:

1. Place one hand on your abdomen and the other on your chest.
2. Breathe naturally and observe which hand moves up and down the most.
3. Take a slow, deep breath through your nose while concentrating on the rise and fall of your abdomen.
4. To understand diaphragmatic breathing, attempt to exaggerate the movement. While inhaling consciously, expand the abdomen, thus forcing the hand up without moving the chest. Then, while exhaling, let the abdomen fall and actually pull it in toward your spine.

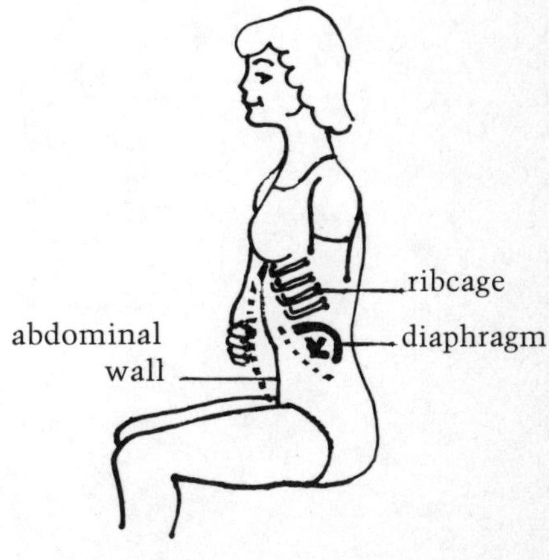

5. Continue deep breathing (without exaggerating) for
   5-10 min while concentrating on the smooth flow of air.
   The abdomen (not the chest!) should rise and fall in the
   deep-breathing pattern.

2. Progressive Relaxation

Progressive Relaxation is a quick tension releaser. Deep
muscle relaxation is achieved through the systematic process
of tensing and relaxing muscles. Once you are able to recog-
nize the feeling and presence of tension, it is much easier to
release it and enjoy its absence.

Sequence:
   1. Lie on your back.
   2. Close your eyes.
   3. Take a few deep breaths and relax.
   4. Now systematically tighten the key muscle groups listed
      below for 5-15 s each. Start with clenching one fist.
      Clench it tightly for 5-15 s until it begins to feel
      uncomfortable. (*Remember*, only your fist should be
      tense, all other muscle groups should be relaxed.) Release
      the tension after 5-15 s and concentrate on the feeling of
      deep relaxation.

Repeat this sequence for each step below:
   1. Clench your right fist tightly for 5-15 s, then relax.
   2. Clench your left fist tightly for 5-15 s, then relax.
   3. Forehead and scalp — raise your eyebrows and ears for
      5-15 s, then relax.
   4. Face — squint your eyes, wrinkle your nose, clench your
      teeth, and pinch your face for 5-15 s, then relax.
   5. Neck — pull your neck towards your chest but don't
      actually touch your chest for 5-15 s, then relax.
   6. Abdomen — take a deep breath and hold, pull in your
      stomach and make it hard for 5-15 s, then relax.

To improve relaxation, you can turn the lights down (or off!) and
listen to soft music. This routine can also be done at the office,
or anywhere else, to relieve stress and tension quickly and effectively; but don't fall asleep. Sleep is not relaxation and will cut
short the learning process.

9/How to Prevent and Treat Common Injuries

The best way to prevent injuries is by using a thorough warm-up before, and a cool-down after exercise. This loosens up each muscle group that you use during your workout. Exercise raises your body temperature, and warm muscles don't tear as easily as cold ones.

Remember: "Train, don't strain." If in doubt, go slower, not faster. Another way to prevent injury is to stop immediately when any exercise becomes painful.

1. Other Safety Habits
— Proper sleeping and eating habits also minimize the risk of injury.
— Avoid icy or slippery conditions.
— Always wear proper workout attire. Use a warm-up suit in cooler weather, which you can take off or put on according to need. There are terrific kinds of winter underwear today, which "wick" the moisture to your outer garment for evaporation, keeping you dry and warm. You should be comfortably warm, never cold, and never too hot during a workout.
— Do not exercise outdoors when it is cold and windy.

2. Common Injuries and How to Treat Them

1. Muscle Stiffness and Soreness
This is a common complaint from anyone starting a fitness programme. Usually the stiffness and soreness are minimal, and by simply lengthening your warm-up and cool-down period, before and after each workout, the symptoms often disappear. A small amount of stiffness is to be expected and indicates that you truly are working your muscles. Anything more than this small amount of soreness and stiffness indicates that you have overdone it. Your best approach now is to have a warm shower or bath or use a heating pad (not hot!), reduce the intensity of

your exercise, or take more rest for the time being. When the stiffness and soreness have disappeared, slowly increase your exercise intensity. Increasing your warm-up and cool-down period whenever muscles are stiff and sore, however, remains the best cure. Often a little *light* exercise of the type that made you sore in the first instance will help get rid of soreness.

2. **Tendonitis**

Tendonitis of the Achilles tendon in the heel is a common injury. When the tendon in this area is overworked, it reacts by becoming inflamed — swollen, hot, and painful. Tendonitis is a more serious condition than muscle stiffness and soreness. It usually occurs in only one joint, whereas muscle stiffness and soreness is felt throughout the whole body. Tendonitis is usually treated by:

1. Resting the sore joint completely, for several days to a week.
2. Applying ice for 15-min periods during the first 24 h and/or
3. Taping, if necessary. If your Achilles tendon, shoulder, or elbow joint becomes particularly painful to move, stop working it for a couple of days. If it is still painful after this rest period, see a physiotherapist or your doctor.

3. **Strained Muscles and Pulls**

Strained or "pulled" muscles are usually the more serious consequence of neglecting muscle stiffness and soreness. They require rest from exercise and, if severe, medical or physiotherapy treatment. Unlike the injuries mentioned earlier, you can usually pinpoint the exact moment a muscle strains or pulls. These injuries are the result of overstressing the muscle and are experienced as a "snapping" or painful pulling sensation. Thorough warm-up and cool-down, as well as avoiding extreme effort, will minimize the chances of straining or pulling your muscles.

10/Nutrition

Dietary requirements vary for each person who has either under-gone heart surgery or had a heart attack. Before leaving the hospital, ask the physician or nutritionist to meet with you and your family to help plan your diet.

The following guide may be helpful in planning your eating habits, once you return home:

> Maintain a well-balanced diet. During the first few weeks following your release from the hospital, eat three or four small meals rather than one or two heavy meals per day.

> Your doctor will tell you if a salt-free diet is required. You should, however, avoid the excessive use of salt as it con-tributes to raising blood pressure.

> All foods supply the body with energy. You will, in your readings, find that there are several methods of measuring, not only the energy that can be taken in by food, but the energy that can be used up through physical activity.

PARTICIPACTION recently published a fitness leaders' kit *The Measure of Energy* that contains the following explanation of kilojoule:

> **The kilojoule** (kJ) is the basic measure of energy. It plays an important role in the fitness context. (Note: The kilojoule is now used in place of the Calorie. It is a smaller unit of measure — one Calorie is equal to about 4.2 kJ). The kilojoule measures all kinds of energy. We might not think that a carrot and running a kilometre have much in common, but, because both food and activity, have energy values, the kilojoule can be used to measure both.

Along with nutrients, all foods contain a certain amount of energy. Different foods have different energy components. For example:

— 1 cooked egg yields 315 kJ
— 1 carrot yields 105 kJ
— 1 slice of cherry pie yields 1470 kJ

Similarly, all human activity involves an expenditure of energy, also measurable in kilojoules. For example, in a 15-min period, a person weighing 70 kg would expend approximately:

— 68 kJ while sleeping
— 95 kJ while eating
— 142 kJ while washing the dishes
— 840 kJ while running

The above examples show us that vigorous physical activity requires a large increase in energy expenditure. The running body uses 10 times more energy than a body at rest. It is this kind of increased energy demand — sustained for relatively short periods of time (15 to 30 min) — that makes fitness and energy grow. To experience a kilojoule of energy try the "kilojoule jump." Standing with your feet slightly apart jump the height you would if you were skipping rope, about 4 to 6 cm. If you weigh between 45 and 55 kg, it will take three jumps to spend one kilojoule. If you weigh between 70 and 90 kg, it will take two jumps to spend one kilojoule. If you weigh between 55 and 70 kg, it's really 2.5 jumps for a kilojoule (think about it on your way down).

You may also run into the word MET (Basal Metabolic Unit) which some exercise leaders use to measure the amount of energy (oxygen) you use during exercise. For example:

    Walking (5 km/h)   = 3.0 METS
    Cycling (19 km/h)   = 9.0 METS

Whatever measurement you use, be sure that you understand it and use it consistently throughout your programme.

Myths About Nutrition

There are many myths associated with nutrition. The following list will help you avoid some common mistakes in planning your diet.

1. *Myth:* "Skipping breakfast is okay because I'm reducing."
    Truth: Skipping meals robs your body of essential nutrients. A balanced breakfast, including protein, grain products, and fruit, improves mental and physical functioning and reduces excessive eating later in the day.

2. *Myth:* "Eating only once a day will help me lose weight."
    Truth: Your body stores less fat if food intake is distributed throughout the day in three to six meals.

3. *Myth:* "Extra protein is required for increased activity."
    Truth: Protein intake above basic requirements does not aid performance. When extra energy is needed for muscle work, it is wiser to increase your intake of carbohydrates such as cereals, breads, and starchy vegetables.

4. *Myth:* "Red meats are the best kind of protein."
    Truth: Many foods other than red meats provide high quality protein. All protein foods are converted to amino acids, which are the building blocks of body tissue. Those with heart problems should rely more on vegetable proteins and can obtain essential amino acids by eating, at the same meal, two or more plant proteins which together provide the essential amino acids. For example:

    > baked beans and bread
    > bean-and-rice casserole
    > bean filling in a corn tortilla

5. *Myth:* "Vitamin supplements provide more energy."
    Truth: Energy does not come from vitamins but from the carbohydrates, fats, and protein in food. Well-planned, well-prepared meals, and snacks supply all the nutrients needed for good health, making vitamin supplements unnecessary, except for certain medical conditions. Self-medication with one or a few vitamins or minerals can lead to an imbalance between nutrients and thereby create even greater problems.

6. *Myth:* "I can rely on thirst to tell me when I need water."
    Truth: You can't. Don't wait that long. Drink at least 4
             glasses of water every day. During long-term
             exercise, 75-100 mL of water every 15-20 min is
             recommended.

7. *Myth:* "Snacking is unhealthy."
    Truth: Snacks can be nutritious. Snacks of raw vegetables,
             low-fat milk products, and grain products can
             prevent fatigue without adding excessive kilojoules.
             Avoid snacks high in fat, salt, sugar, and caffeine.

8. *Myth:* "The only salt I have to worry about is that which I
             add to my food."
    Truth: High salt intake can contribute to high blood
             pressure in genetically susceptible individuals.
             Limit the amount of salt you add to foods, but also
             read package labels because salt (sodium) is
             commonly added to many foods. Also avoid
             processed foods (e.g., pre-packed cold cuts, soups,
             etc.).

11/Conclusion

Next to the Introduction, the concluding remarks are always the most difficult to write. There are, however, a few general comments that might be helpful.

One of the key facts to be aware of is how depressed your physical state will be, especially after your release from the hospital. There will not be a lot of energy reserve left in the body. If you don't realize this, you may have a tendency to push yourself harder just to prove to yourself and others that nothing has really happened. This would be a mistake as you have nothing to prove to your friends or yourself.

Begin to take control of your life. Learn to say NO if an activity or event does not coincide with your new lifestyle of proper nutrition, exercise, rest, and recreation, all balanced with mental and physical relaxation.

Prior to taking part in an activity, you may want to practise in order to determine just how draining it will be, both mentally and physically. For example, you may want to practise going to work so that you will have a realistic understanding of the demands that will be placed on you.

Finally, it is our hope that this book will help in raising your confidence level and that you will be much more active than you first thought you could be after your heart attack or surgery. Most of all, it is our hope that your increased awareness of physical fitness and a change in your lifestyle will help you take even more positive control of your life.

Good Luck and Good Health.

Appendices

Resources

Most large hospitals and local university hospitals will have cardiac units and provide advice and counselling on dealing with rehabilitation programmes.

The Canadian Heart and Lung Association, The Canadian Red Cross, and the Canadian Medical Association should all have helpful information for those in need of guidance. Most of these organizations have offices in major cities across Canada. The network of PARTICIPACTION across the country is also a good source of information and programmes. Your own family doctor will also have many leads to counselling for you.

Glossary

Aerobic exercise:	Exercise during which the energy is provided by metabolism requiring oxygen.
Anaerobic Exercise:	Exercise during which the energy needed is provided by metabolic reactions in absence of oxygen.
Aneurysm:	A spindle-shaped or sac-like bulging wall of a vein or artery, caused by weakening of the walls.
Angina:	Chest pains caused by lack of blood flow to the heart.
Anoxia:	Lack of oxygen.
Arrhythmia:	Abnormal rhythm of the heart beat.
Arteriosclerosis:	Commonly called hardening of the arteries.
Atrophy:	Reduction in size of a structure.
Blood Pressure:	The pressure of the blood in the arteries:
	Systolic: The pressure in the artery as the blood leaves the heart.
	Diastolic: Pressure in the artery in between the strokes.
Bradycardia:	Slow heart rate (below 60 beats per minute)
Calorie:	Unit formerly used for measuring the value of foods for producing heat and energy in the human body. See *kilojoule*.
Cardiac Cycle:	One total heart beat.
Catheterization:	Examination of the heart by introducing a thin tube into a vein or artery and passing it into the heart.
Cholesterol:	Fatlike susbstance found in animal tissue. High levels associated with heart disease.
Dyspnea:	Difficult or laboured breathing.
Electrocardiogram:	Called EKG or ECG, is a graphic record of the electric currents produced by the heart.
Hypertension:	High blood pressure.
Isometric:	Exercise without movement, e.g., trying to raise a window that is stuck.
Isotonic:	Exercise with dynamic movement, i.e., walking, swimming, bicycling.
Kilojoule:	Unit for measuring energy used in place of the calorie — 1 kJ is slightly less than 0.25 calories.

MET: Basal metabolic unit — Metabolic
                        equivalent (multiple of resting metabolism
                        = 3.5 mL $0^1/_2$/kg/min.)
Myocardial   Damage to an area of the heart muscle
  Infarction: caused by lack of blood flow to that area.
Open-Heart   Surgery performed on the open heart while
  Surgery: the blood stream is diverted through a
                        heart-lung machine.
Saturated Fat: Solid fats of animal origin, such as the fats
                        in milk, butter, meats, etc.; a diet of which
                        tends to increase the amount of cholesterol
                        in the blood.

Energy Value of Some Common Foods

Food	Measure		kJ	Calories
Milk, whole (3.5% fat)	250 mL	1 cup	660	160
Milk, skim	250 mL	1 cup	380	90
Milk, partially skimmed (2%)	250 mL	1 cup	540	123
Cocoa (with whole milk)	250 mL	1 cup	960	245
Cola	365 mL	12 oz	610	145
Tea or coffee (black, no sugar)			0	0
Butter or margarine	15 mL	1 tbsp	420	100
Mayonnaise	15 mL	1 tbsp	420	100
Salad dressing, French (regular)	15 mL	1 tbsp	250	59
Yoghurt, plain (partially skimmed milk)	100 mL	6 oz	360	112
Cheddar cheese (2.5 cm cube)	30 g	1 oz	466	116
Swiss cheese, processed, Gruyere	30 g	1 oz	420	115
Eggs, large, raw or cooked	1 egg		330	80
Ground beef, broiled	90 g	3 oz	1080	245
Steak, broiled, relatively fat	90 g	3 oz	1330	330
Steak, broiled, lean only	90 g	3 oz	690	175
Stewing beef or pot roast, lean and fat	90 g	3 oz	1420	339
Bacon, side, fried crisp	2 slices		380	90
Pork chop, lean and fat	70 g	2.3 oz	1090	260
Liver, beef, fried	60 g	2 oz	574	130
Chicken breast, flesh and skin	80 g	2.7 oz	650	155
Luncheon meats	60 g	2 oz	740	165
Halibut, grilled with butter	90 g	3 oz	640	146
Ocean perch, breaded, fried	90 g	3 oz	840	195
Salmon, fried in butter	90 g	3 oz	680	155
Tuna, canned, solids only	90 g	3 oz	740	170
Asparagus, green, cooked, drained	4 spears		40	10
Beans, green or yellow, cooked	250 mL	1 cup	130	30
Beets, cooked, diced or sliced	250 mL	1 cup	240	55
Brussels sprouts, cooked	250 mL	1 cup	240	55
Cabbage, cooked finely shredded	250 mL	1 cup	150	35
Carrots, raw, whole	1 carrot		80	20
Cauliflower, cooked	250 mL	1 cup	130	25
Corn, sweet, cooked	1 ear		290	70
Lettuce, raw, leaves	2 large		40	10
Onions, raw	1 onion		170	40
Peas, green, cooked	250 mL	1 cup	510	115

Energy Value of Some Common Foods

Food	Measure	kJ	Calories
Potatoes, baked and peeled	1 potato	380	90
Potatoes, French fried in deep fat	10 pieces	650	155
Potato chips	10 chips	480	115
Spinach, cooked	250 mL 1 cup	180	40
Tomatoes, raw	1 tomato	150	35
Turnips, cooked, cubes	125 mL 1/2 cup	160	35
Apples, raw	1 apple	290	70
Apple sauce, canned, sweetened	1 cup	1020	230
Bananas, raw	1 banana	420	100
Grapefruit, raw, medium	1/2 g'fruit	190	45
Grapes, raw, Canadian type	30 grapes	270	106
Oranges, raw	1 orange	270	65
Peaches, raw, medium	1 peach	150	35
Raspberries, raw	250 mL 1 cup	310	70
Bread, white, enriched	1 slice	340	82
Bread, whole wheat, 60%	1 slice	300	72
Cornflakes, plain	250 mL 1 cup	280	80
Oatmeal cookies	1 biscuit	360	86
Doughnuts, cake type	1	520	125
Pie, pumpkin	1 piece	1330	320

Bibliography

Type A Behavior and Your Heart, Friedman, M. and Rosenman, R. Fawcett Crest, New York, 1975.

Heart Attack? Counter Attack! Kavanaugh, T. T. Van Nostrand Reinhold Publishing, 1976.

Adult Fitness and Cardiac Rehabilitation, Wilson, P. University Park Press, Baltimore, 1975.

Stress Without Distress, Selye, H. J.B. Lippincott, New York.

Stretching, Anderson, B. Shelter Publications, Bolinas, California, 1980.